ACTIVITIES TO DEVELOP LEARNING SKILLS AT KS3

Helen Sonnet and Cassandra Sonnet

Permission to photocopy

This book contains materials which may be reproduced by photocopier or other means for use by the purchaser. The permission is granted on the understanding that these copies will be used within the educational establishment of the purchaser. The book and all its contents remain copyright. Copies may be made without reference to the publisher or the licensing scheme for the making of photocopies operated by the Publishers Licensing Agency.

The rights of Helen Sonnet and Cassandra Sonnet to be identified as the authors of this work have been asserted by them in accordance with sections 77 and 78 of the Copyright, Designs and Patents Act.

Activities to Develop Learning Skills at KS3
ISBN: 978-1-85503-564-5

© Helen Sonnet and Cassandra Sonnet
Illustrations by Bethan Matthews and Tony Forbes/Sylvie Poggio Artists
(Bethan Matthews: pp. 131, 132, 134, 135, 140, 141; Tony Forbes: pp. 126, 139, 143)

All rights reserved
First published 2014
Printed in the UK for LDA
LDA, Findel Education, 2 Gregory Street, Hyde, Cheshire SK14 4HR

Contents

Introduction   7

Learning at Key Stage 3 8

Describing   11

The tiniest detail 12
Describe and draw 13
Five sentences 14
My object 15
A minute to win it 16
Who am I? 17
Three words.. 18

Retrieving   19

Spot the detail 20
I went to the zoo 21
Missing numbers 22
What's in a tale? 23
A back-to-front day 25
What did I do? 27
Whose favourite pudding? 28

Identifying   29

Through asking 30
Odd one out 31
Wanted 32
A mirror image? 33
What am I? 34
What's the sound? 36
Think of an animal 37

CONTENTS

Understanding — 38

- Consequences — 39
- What's the question? — 40
- Making sense — 41
- Because… — 43
- Check the context — 44
- Why did? — 45
- Statement, question, answer — 46

Interpreting — 48

- What's in a dream? — 49
- Interpret the sign — 50
- Mime requests — 51
- Why is the dog tied to the railings? — 52
- Interpreting symbols — 53
- Idioms — 54
- Cockney rhyming slang — 56

Collating — 58

- When did it happen? — 59
- Categorise and collate — 60
- Story sequence — 61
- Oldest to youngest — 62
- Rules of the school — 63
- Colours of the rainbow — 64
- Which word comes first? — 65

Refining — 66

- Short and sweet — 67
- Smiley faces — 68
- The sum total — 69
- Wishes — 70
- Too much talk — 71
- Desert island list — 73
- Refine and unrefine — 74

Inferring · 75

Where am I? 76
Who and what? 78
What can you deduce? 80
Faces 81
What's happened? 82
What is going on? 83
Who would wear that? 84

Analysing · 85

Guess what I am 86
The sum of many parts 88
Study the picture 89
Riddles 90
Who likes what? 92
Sort them out 93
Spot the difference 94

Evaluating · 95

Likes/dislikes 96
The best advert 97
What's the most important? 98
I would rather 99
The best present 100
The best headteacher 101
Gobbledegook 102

Investigating · 103

Who walked on my flowerbed? 104
Legends 105
Find the facts 106
What's the story? 107
All boys like football 108
Investigative questions 109
Which country? 110

CONTENTS

Exploring — 111

Design a set 112
What's in a name? 113
Abstract art 114
Discover the message 115
Who saved the day? 116
What a disaster! 117
What happened next? 118

Projects — 119

A suitable timetable 120
Creating a children's TV programme 121
A summer event 122
The town council project 123
Designer drink 124

Photocopiable resources — 125

INTRODUCTION

INTRODUCTION

Learning at Key Stage 3

Key Stage 3 can be regarded as a somewhat tricky and unfocused period of teaching – three years that some see as nothing more than a transitory period between the basic learning at primary school and the independence and rigour of Key Stage 4. Indeed, teacher assessments and judgements will always be viewed as a less robust and concrete method of assessment than the nationwide examinations and coursework that pupils encounter during their GCSEs. This can lead to teaching at Key Stage 3 taking a back seat in terms of preparation, feedback and development, especially if teachers are also teaching classes of Year 10 and 11 pupils where the focus is on their GCSE grades, the reflection of these as a whole on the school and their importance to league tables. These older students are thought of as being 'the ones who count' and therefore Key Stage 3 pupils can sometimes find themselves a lesser priority for a time-poor teacher speeding flat out to the summer exam season, or preparing for modular tests that occur more frequently than rainy summer days.

Key Stage 3 can seem like the prolonging of primary teaching, especially if the first two years of Key Stage 3 are taught in a middle school. Similarly, some schools separate Key Stage 3 and 4 pupils on split sites or in different buildings, and often this is accompanied by separate teachers. To raise standards at Key Stage 4, Key Stage 3 teachers must be made aware of the skills needed to succeed at GCSE level and begin to apply them within their own teaching. This will help develop continuity throughout a pupil's education and make the leap from Key Stage 3 to 4 less daunting.

It is precisely because Key Stage 3 is not so pressured that it allows a tremendous amount of scope to prepare students for GCSE learning. Because the curriculum is not so intense, there may be more time to focus on the teaching of learning skills that set pupils up as independent and evaluative learners both during Key Stage 3 and at Key Stage 4. Pupils who are made aware of their own learning are much more able to reflect on their progression and can decide meaningful and progressive targets to help them move forward.

INTRODUCTION

Much of Key Stage 3 assessment is based on seeing how well pupils are doing in relation to their prior attainment, and in comparison with other pupils their own age. Again, this can lead to teaching becoming restricted and focusing on looking backwards, or sideways at others, rather than forwards in anticipation of GCSEs. However, Key Stage 3 can be so much more than this; if the time is used wisely teachers can still fulfil their duties of judgement and assessment but can also prepare students for progression at Key Stage 4 and thus raise overall attainment.

As at GCSE, there is a sliding scale of learning criteria at Key Stage 3. The headings in this book are taken from the Key Stage 3 descriptors across all relevant subjects. They follow the basic principles of skills progression – from simple understanding at one end to the independence of original evaluation at the other – with the idea that pupils can move on from one to the next once confidence has been built in each area. The activities vary in terms of how long they take to complete – some can be used as a five-minute interlude in a lesson to clarify a learning skill, while others are suited to a half or a whole lesson. There are also several projects at the end of the book that take a succession of lessons to complete. These projects are not subject-specific and may be used within the pastoral system, but each one includes many of the descriptors and is developed in such a way that pupils can see progression and mastery of the skills as the project is completed.

All pupils, regardless of their level of attainment, benefit from self-assurance in the classroom, ownership of their own learning and awareness of how to progress. The skills in this book aim to develop within pupils the ability to access the curriculum and to succeed within the school environment. Self-confidence and conviction are just as important as academic achievement when it comes to succeeding beyond the school walls, and enjoyment of the learning process will go some way towards engagement with the education system as a whole.

DESCRIBING

Describing is a straightforward learning skill whereby the student is able to tell, or give an account of, any given thing using the spoken or written word. Many students can be brief when using description, so these activities aim to develop a student's ability to describe something in greater depth. Detail is rewarded; students will therefore see the merit in extending their descriptions to give as thorough and comprehensive an answer as possible.

DESCRIBING

The tiniest detail

This activity encourages the students to examine objects closely and pay attention to every detail.

 Group size: Pairs

 Time: 10–30 minutes

 Resources: A selection of objects; for example sellotape dispenser, watch, toy, toothbrush

What to do

Put the students into pairs and give each pair an object. Explain that they are to take turns to describe the object one point at a time. They can describe the appearance, nature or attributes of the object, but not its origins. For example, if the object was a rolling pin, they might say, 'It is cylindrical', 'It has two handles', 'It is wooden', 'It is used for rolling out pastry', but they couldn't say, 'It comes from a tree'. The aim of the activity is to have the last word and score a point. They can continue with as many different objects as time allows.

Variation

You can also use this activity with photographs of houses, places of interest and people cut out of magazines.

DESCRIBING

Describe and draw

This activity is a straightforward example of awareness of detail in relayed information.

Group size: 5–6

Time: 20–30 minutes

Resources: For each group, a set of the drawings on the photocopiable sheet *Describe and draw* (p. 126), cut up and placed face down in a pack; paper and pencils

What to do

Each group sits in a circle. One player from each group picks up the top card from the pack and turns it over, making sure that no one else in the group can see the picture (it may be a good idea to provide a book or similar object to hold in front of the photocopied picture, obscuring it from the view of the other players). They describe the drawing in detail and the other players make a drawing based on the details that they hear. The player whose drawing is the closest match to the original gets a point. If several are equally close, they all receive a point. The next player picks up a new picture and repeats the process. The activity continues until all players have had a turn or you run out of time.

Extension

The students take turns to sit outside the circle and construct a simple drawing. This could be a pattern or an object. They describe what they are doing as they add each detail and the other players make a drawing based on this description. The player whose drawing most closely matches the original scores a point.

DESCRIBING

Five sentences

This encourages the students to think of effective descriptions that will convey the most important information.

 Group size: 5–6

 Time: 30 minutes

 Resources: Paper and pencils

What to do

Give each group a topic; for example making a cup of tea, *The X Factor*, Christmas Day or a topical film such as the most recent James Bond movie. The students in each group must write five sentences about their topic. They must do this individually without conferring with other members of their group. Explain that the object of this activity is to convey as much information as clearly as possible in just five sentences. For lower-attaining groups, you might want to reduce this number to three. Each group then joins up with another group. The players in the first group take turns to read their sentences to the second group, who vote on the best set of sentences that they feel tells them the most about the given topic. They explain the reasons for their choice; for example clarity, scope. The groups then reverse roles.

Extension

Give each group a new topic and ask the players to write just one sentence conveying the most important aspect of that topic. Let them compare sentences to see how many chose the same aspect. They get one point if they were the only player, two points if two players chose the same aspect, three points if three players chose the same aspect, and so on.

DESCRIBING

My object

The students are encouraged to focus on details in their descriptions of objects in order to convey relevant information.

 Group size: Individual

 Time: 20–30 minutes

 Resources: A selection of objects; an open box with a cloth cover

What to do

The students take turns to describe an object hidden from view inside a box. They must not name the object. The remaining students try to guess the identity of the object.

Variation

Collect photos of food, celebrities, sports, animals, and so on, from magazines. Ask for a volunteer and attach a photo to their back with sticky tape. The volunteer turns around to show the other players the photo. They ask questions until they guess the photo. For example, if the photo is of an animal they might ask questions such as 'Am I large/small?', 'How many legs do I have?', 'What colour am I?', 'Where do I live?', 'What do I eat?' Encourage them to consider the details that would help them to guess their photo and then ask the appropriate questions.

DESCRIBING

A minute to win it

This activity encourages the students to look for the smallest details in order to prolong their descriptions.

Group size: 5–6

Time: 15–20 minutes

Resources: A list of the same objects for each group; for example a kettle, a ham sandwich, a car, a television; a stopwatch or watch with a second hand for each group

What to do

Explain to the students that they are each going to choose an object from the list. They will take it in turns to describe their object while being timed, and attempt to talk for one minute. Tell the students that the more detail they are able to include in their speech, the longer they will be able to talk. Allow a minute before starting the activity for the students to study their objects and think about what they will say.

Extension

Find the champion describer with a second-round contest. The student from each group who was able to talk about their object the longest chooses a new object to describe.

DESCRIBING

Who am I?

The students must describe themselves in as much detail as possible in order to provide the necessary clues for the others to guess their identity.

 Group size: Whole class

 Time: 15 minutes

 Resources: Paper and pencils

What to do

Explain to the students that they are going to write descriptions of themselves in as much detail as possible, including their appearance, character, likes and dislikes. They must not show anyone their descriptions. These are folded and put into a container. The students take turns to pull out a paper and read the description for the others to guess the identity of the student. Discuss with the students if any particular details were more important than others.

Extension

Ask the students to describe a famous person, including as much detail as possible for the others to guess their identity.

DESCRIBING

Three words

The students consider a selection of adjectives to decide which provide the best descriptions.

 Group size: 3–4

 Time: 10–15 minutes

 Resources: Two or three interesting photographs from magazines/journals; paper and pencils; whiteboard and pen

What to do

Explain to the students that you are going to show them photographs. Within their groups they must write down words that describe the photographs and then choose just three that they think best describe the scene. Write the words from each group on the whiteboard and take a vote on the whole-class choices for the best three.

Extension

Discuss with the class the aspects that they focus on in choosing their words, such as the physical attributes of the scene, what is happening and what emotions are present.

RETRIEVING

The ability to retrieve information is a basic but vital skill for success in education. At its simplest level, retrieval is the reproduction of taught material, and the ability to recover or regain knowledge. It does not require the more complex thinking skills of higher Key Stage 3 descriptors, but the ability to retrieve is a fundamental building block of learning. These activities will show students that they can retain knowledge and reproduce it.

RETRIEVING

Spot the detail

This activity requires a concentrated visual focus to help the students retrieve the necessary information.

 Group size: Individual

 Time: 10 minutes

 Resources: A photograph or picture with lots of detail; a prepared set of questions based on the photograph/picture; paper and pencils (optional)

What to do

Choose a photograph from a magazine or a picture that contains plenty of detail. For example, you might take a photograph from a travel brochure or a school reference book. Prepare a set of questions of varying difficulty, such as: 'What colour was the car in the foreground?', 'How many buses were parked at the bus stop?', 'What was the dog doing?', 'Who was sitting on the park bench?', 'Was the fountain on the left- or right-hand side of the picture?' The picture needs to be large enough for all the class to see and you might want to call the students to the front of the classroom. Explain that they are going to study the picture for one minute, after which you will ask questions about it. They need to try and take in as much detail as possible, such as how many, what colour, where things are situated. After a minute, turn the picture over and ask the prepared set of questions. The students can either write down their answers or can answer as a class with a show of hands.

Variation

Photocopy a busy picture for each student or for pairs of students. Ask questions about the picture and see who is the first to respond with the correct answer.

I went to the zoo

The students must listen and concentrate in order to retrieve items in a list from their memories.

 Group size: 6–8 or whole class

 Time: 15–20 minutes

 Resources: None

What to do

This activity can either be played in small groups or as a whole class. Small groups would be easier for lower-attaining students, as there will be fewer items to remember, at least for their first turn. The students sit in a circle and one begins by saying, 'I went to the zoo and saw…', naming an animal, for example a zebra. The student next to them repeats the opening and adds a new animal: 'I went to the zoo and saw a zebra and an elephant.' The activity continues in this way with each student repeating what the previous student has said and then adding a new animal to the list, until someone is unable to remember all the animals. This student then starts a new list. Other lists could be: I went to the seaside and saw…, I went to the shops and bought….

Extension

Higher-attaining students could add details to their list; for example, 'I went to the zoo and saw a camel with a wonky ear, a tiger with green stripes, a three-legged elephant and a gorilla with bushy eyebrows.'

RETRIEVING

Missing numbers

The students retrieve a list from memory to spot the missing item.

 Group size: Individual

 Time: 10–15 minutes

 Resources: A list of number sequences; paper and pencils; whiteboard and pen

What to do

Write a sequence of numbers on the whiteboard and say them at the same time. (Begin with three or four numbers and then increase this as the students become more adept at spotting the missing number.) Erase the numbers, then rewrite them and say the list, omitting one number. Ask the students to write down the missing number. You can use a number more than once in a sequence.

Variation

Repeat the activity using letters in place of numbers.

What's in a tale?

The students listen to a short narrative and answer questions on it.

 Group: Individual

 Time: 15 minutes

 Resources: Paper and pencils

What to do

Read the text below in a fairly slow manner, giving the students time to digest the details, and then ask the questions that follow. The students write down their answers.

> Archie came to call for me at nine o'clock. I was still eating my breakfast of porridge at the time, so Archie joined me at the table and ate a piece of toast. We were catching the number 25 bus, which stops right outside my front gate at nine fifteen and going to the local pool to swim. The bus was ten minutes late and, as it was a really cold morning, Archie and I had to stamp our feet and blow on our hands to try and keep warm. As we boarded the bus, I saw grumpy old Mrs Kenton with her red tartan shopping trolley sitting near to the front. We sat well behind her so that she did not see us, as she would be sure to start grumbling about kids playing football outside her flat. At the pool we quickly changed and jumped into the warm, blue water. One half of the pool had three roped-off lanes for those people who wanted to swim up and down but the remainder was open. We spent over an hour jumping and diving underwater and generally messing about. I was really embarrassed back in the changing room, when I realised that mum had packed my sister's pink towel instead of my blue one. Archie had a good laugh at my expense and threatened to tell everyone in school. We went into the pool's café and I had a hot chocolate and Archie had a coke. We both had jam doughnuts as well – swimming always makes me so hungry.

RETRIEVING

Questions

1. What time did Archie call for the narrator?
2. What was the narrator eating for breakfast?
3. What did Archie eat?
4. What number bus did the boys catch?
5. Where did the bus stop?
6. What time was the bus due?
7. How late was the bus?
8. What colour was Mrs Kenton's shopping trolley?
9. How many lanes were roped off for swimmers?
10. How long did the boys spend in the pool?
11. Why was the narrator embarrassed after his swim?
12. What did Archie drink in the café?
13. What did the narrator drink in the café?
14. What did both boys eat in the café?

Extension

Try reading extracts from different types of text; for example a holiday brochure, an adventure story, a technical manual or a collector's journal, to see if the students are more able to retain information from one type of text than another. Discuss with the students why this might be; for example, they might find some text more interesting and remain focused for longer or other text may contain words that they are unfamiliar with and therefore unable to remember.

RETRIEVING

A back-to-front day

The students need to retrieve information from their memories and present it in the reverse order.

 Group size: Individual

 Time: 20 minutes

 Resources: Paper and pencils

What to do

Read the sentences below that outline incidents in someone's day. Ask the students to rewrite the day in the reverse order, i.e. they begin with the final action and end with the first incident.

1. The alarm clock woke me at 7.30am.
2. I went to the bathroom, washed and cleaned my teeth.
3. I went downstairs to the kitchen where I ate a breakfast of toast and jam.
4. I caught the 8.30am bus to school.
5. My first lesson at school was English.
6. At break time I ate an apple and drank water.
7. After break I had science.
8. Before lunch, my lesson was maths.
9. At lunchtime I ate a sandwich of cheese and pickle, a yoghurt and a banana.
10. I walked home with my friend Ally and we played on his Xbox for an hour.
11. I ate chilli con carne for tea followed by rhubarb crumble and ice cream.

RETRIEVING

12. I watched an adventure film and went to bed at 9pm.

You may want to reduce the number of incidents with lower-attaining groups.

Variation

Read out a recipe from a cookery book and ask the students to rewrite it in the reverse order.

What did I do?

The students must try and remember a sequence of movements to replicate them.

Group size: Whole class and pairs

Time: 20 minutes

Resources: Paper and pencils

What to do

Ask the students to watch you closely as you carry out the sequence of movements below.

> Touch your knees, then shoulders, clap twice, turn on the spot, raise your arms above your head, then out to the side, march on the spot, turn around again, crouch and touch the floor, do a star jump, raise your right arm, raise your left arm, turn on the spot and crouch down.

Let the students take turns to try and complete the same sequence of movements. Ask them to study the next sequence and all try to replicate it.

> Stand with your feet apart, jump to bring your feet together, hop twice on your right foot, touch your right hand to your left foot, turn around, bring both hands out to the side then above your head, touch your left hand to your right foot, turn around, hop twice on your left foot, swing your right arm in an anti-clockwise direction, clasp your hands behind back, crouch down and touch the floor, jump up and finish with your feet apart.

Extension

Put the students into pairs. Ask them each to write out a sequence of movements. They take turns to perform their sequences for their partners to copy.

RETRIEVING

Whose favourite pudding?

The students must try and remember who voted for which pudding.

 Group size: Whole class

 Time: 10 minutes

 Resources: Whiteboard and pen

What to do

Write the names of six puddings on the whiteboard; for example ice cream, apple pie, fruit crumble, sticky toffee pudding, cheesecake, chocolate sponge. Saying each pudding in turn, ask the students to raise their hands if it is their favourite from the list. They can only choose one. Name the students aloud for each choice. When you have completed the list, pick one of the puddings and ask for a volunteer to try and name all the students who chose that particular one. When the student has finished, ask if anyone who made that choice was not named. Repeat with the other puddings.

Extension

Repeat with a different category, such as sweets. Ask the students to write down the names for each choice (they could just write initials to save time). Run through the list and ask the students to raise their hands when you name their favourite. The students receive a point for each person correctly named under each sweet. Find out who has the highest score.

IDENTIFYING

A student is able to identify when they can recognise or verify the identity of a person or thing. This builds on the learning skill of retrieval. These activities aim to encourage students to use their knowledge to identify certain aspects of new and unseen material. The ability to identify is a learning skill that encourages a student to be aware of progression and development as they can see, very simply, that previous teaching enables present and future understanding.

IDENTIFYING

Through asking

This teaches the students how to discover and establish particular aspects of a person.

Group size: Individual

Time: 30 minutes

Resources: For each student, a copy of the photocopiable sheet *Through asking* (p. 127); pencils

What to do

Give each student a copy of the list and explain that they must walk around the room, talk to the other students and fill in the details on the sheet as quickly as possible. At regular intervals, stop the activity to ask how many questions they have completed. When time runs out or someone has finished, call the students together and work through the list asking for volunteers to provide their answers. With lower-attaining groups, you may want to shorten or simplify the list.

Extension

Ask the students to imagine that they are creating a document for each person that will be completely unique to them. What features would they include to ensure that the document could only identify the person specified?

IDENTIFYING

Odd one out

The students try and identify the odd one out from a list of words.

 Group size: Pairs or individual

 Time: 10 minutes

 Resources: Paper and pencils

What to do

Read slowly each of the lists of words below twice and ask the students to identify and write down the odd word that does not belong in each group.

1. Poodle, labrador, <u>turpin</u>, wolfhound, dalmatian
2. Euro, dollar, yen, <u>wingo</u>
3. Spade, <u>rowel</u>, shears, dibber, fork
4. <u>Croach</u>, tench, perch, trout, pike
5. Radish, courgette, <u>carob</u>, cucumber, lettuce
6. Ghost, horror, adventure, <u>sleepy</u>, thriller
7. Peony, daffodil, narcissus, <u>stilia</u>, foxglove
8. Buffalo, antelope, yak, gnu, <u>lek</u>
9. Iceland, Greenland, <u>Snowland</u>, Finland, Lapland
10. Greenfinch, <u>bluefinch</u>, chaffinch, bullfinch, goldfinch

Extension

Ask the groups to compose a list of items with an odd one out and let each group call out their list for the other students to identify the incorrect word.

IDENTIFYING

Wanted

This activity demonstrates how we identify others by recognising their features.

 Group size: Pairs

 Time: 30 minutes

 Resources: Magazine photos of celebrities brought in by the students – these can be musicians, singers, actors, sports personalities; paper and pencils

What to do

Paste the photos onto card and give each a number. Display them around the classroom. Give each pair of students a piece of paper and a pencil and tell them to write the numbers 1– (however many photos you have). Ask them to walk round the room, looking at the photos and identifying as many celebrities as they can. Ask them to write the name of the celebrity alongside the appropriate number. When time has run out or a pair has completed their list, call the students together and identify each celebrity. Discuss with the students how they recognise other individuals. Repeat this process on a different occasion with only the eyes of each celebrity displayed, and compare the success rate of correct identification with the first activity. Discuss the possible reasons for the results.

Variation

In the follow-up activity, you could cut each face into quarters and make composite faces from four different celebrities, then ask the students if they are able to identify all four people involved.

IDENTIFYING

A mirror image?

The students have to use their looking and concentrating skills to identify differences in patterns.

Group size: Individual

Time: 30+ minutes

Resources: Graph paper; pencils; rulers

What to do

Give each student a piece of graph paper, a pencil and a ruler. Ask them to draw a rectangle and divide it in half vertically. Explain that they are going to draw a pattern or picture in the left half of the rectangle and its mirror image in the right half. However, they are going to make a deliberate mistake in the mirror image. Once the students have completed this, they show their drawings to other students to see who can spot the deliberate mistake.

Extension

The students repeat the activity, but they rotate the mirror image 90 degrees to make it more difficult to spot the mistake.

IDENTIFYING

What am I?

This activity encourages the students to focus on a set of features in order to identify an object.

 Group size: Individual

 Time: 15–20 minutes

 Resources: Paper and pencils

What to do

Give each student a piece of paper and a pencil. Ask them to write the numbers 1–5 on the left-hand side. Read out the sets of sentences below for each of the objects, one at a time. Ask the students to guess the identity of the object that you are describing after each sentence. Their identification may change throughout the activity, sometimes with each set of features. When you have completed the sentences, tell the students the correct identity. They score points for correct identification on a sliding scale. If they correctly identified the object after the first sentence, they score five points. If they made the correct identification after the second sentence, they score four points. After the third sentence, they score three points, and so on. Discuss with the students why correct identification became easier after each sentence to establish the fact that an increasing number of features provided more clues to help them guess.

A. 1. I am white and cuboid.
   2. I am found in homes.
   3. I have a door in my front.
   4. I am attached to electric and water supplies.
   5. You can view my insides through a circular window in my door.

   What am I? *A washing machine.*

IDENTIFYING

B. 1. I am produced for a certain celebration.
   2. I am often covered in something soft and sweet.
   3. I can be round, square or the shape of an object.
   4. Sometimes I have writing on top of me.
   5. Usually I have candles on top of me.

   What am I? *A birthday cake.*

C. 1. I am made of metal, plastic and material.
   2. I have many doors and windows.
   3. I have many seats.
   4. I am used to carry people from one place to another.
   5. I run on tracks.

   What am I? *A train.*

Extension

Put the students into pairs and ask them to choose an object and write a similar set of five sentences for others to guess.

IDENTIFYING

What's the sound?

This activity focuses on the use of listening skills in identification.

Group size: Pairs or groups of 3

Time: 20 minutes

Resources: Sounds of instruments – these can be found on the internet at www.sfskids.org or www.philharmonia.co.uk; paper and pencils

What to do

Give each pair/group paper and a pencil. Explain that you are going to play the sounds of different instruments to them and they must try and guess the identity of each instrument. Play the sounds, one at a time, allowing a minute or so for discussion and writing. When you have completed this, repeat the sounds and correctly identify each instrument. Discuss with the students the importance of good listening skills; for example to identify people's voices, to hear the sounds of potential danger such as an approaching vehicle, and to gather important information.

Variation

Record the voices of all the staff at your school repeating the same sentence and play the recording to the students to see how many voices they can correctly identify.

IDENTIFYING

Think of an animal

The students must think of appropriate questions to ask in order to help them identify different animals.

 Group size: 6

 Time: 10–15 minutes

 Resources: None

What to do

The students take turns within their groups to think of an animal. The other members of the group ask pertinent questions until they are able to identify the animal correctly.

Variation

This activity can be played many times with different categories; for example dinners, sweets, TV celebrities/programmes.

UNDERSTANDING

Understanding is the key to developing a personal response to taught material. Students start to think independently about what has been taught and use their mental processes to synthesise information. Understanding is the first step towards the mastery of higher-order thinking skills and is the foundation on which learning is built. If a student is made aware of their ability to understand, they will soon realise that they can succeed in school. These activities aim to encourage students to think independently about what has been taught.

UNDERSTANDING

Consequences

The students show that they understand actions have consequences as they explore the many possible outcomes.

 Group size: 6

 Time: 10–15 minutes

 Resources: Whiteboard and pen

What to do

Write up the following sentences on the whiteboard:

- The football crashed through the lounge window shattering the glass into a thousand pieces.
- She smuggled the kitten past the kitchen where her parents were sat drinking tea and up to her bedroom.
- The boy saw the man slip the DVD inside his coat and walk out of the shop without paying.
- Marlin heard that Shoniece had called him an unkind name.

Explain to the students that they are each to think of a possible consequence that might occur after each incident and discuss this within their groups.

Extension

Choose one of the situations to discuss with the whole class. After listening to the possible outcomes the students offer, ask them if they consider that one is more likely to happen and why.

UNDERSTANDING

What's the question?

The students demonstrate understanding by thinking of pertinent questions.

 Group size: 6

 Time: 10–15 minutes

 Resources: Whiteboard and pen

What to do

Write the following sentences on the whiteboard:

- I'll have the melon, thanks.
- It's about 2.30.
- I didn't know you were there.
- It fell out of a tree.
- It's the blue one over there.

Ask the students to think of as many questions as they can within their groups that would prompt each of the above responses. Discuss with the students how analysis of text is important to aid understanding, in this case to think of suitable questions.

Extension

Choose one or two of the responses and discuss their questions with the whole class. Did the groups devise similar questions to each other? Was there a particular question that every group thought of?

UNDERSTANDING

Making sense

The students have to show understanding by making sense of a jumbled conversation.

Group size: Pairs

Time: 10 minutes

Resources: For each pair, a copy of the jumbled conversation on the photocopiable sheet *Making sense* (p. 128); pencils

What to do

Explain to the students that they have been given a jumbled conversation. They must work out the conversation and put the sentences into the correct order by numbering them from 1 onwards. The conversation should read as follows:

'Hello, you're back from holiday then?'

'Oh hi. Yes, we got home yesterday afternoon.'

'Where did you go?'

'We went to India.'

'You must have seen some fabulous sights there.'

'Yes, there are many beautiful temples and everything is very colourful.'

'Yes, especially the brightly coloured spices. Did you find the food too spicy?'

'Oh no, I love hot curries.'

'Just as well, otherwise you might have got very hungry.'

'All that talk of being hungry has made me feel hungry! Do you want to go and have some lunch?'

'Good idea. Where shall we go?'

UNDERSTANDING

'Nico's does really tasty baguettes.'

'I prefer The Lemon Tree as I like the cakes there.'

'Okay, that's where we'll go.'

Extension

Discuss with the whole class what helped them to understand the conversation; for example picking out key words in the questions and answers.

UNDERSTANDING

Because…

The students are asked to think of places to visit and reasons for going there.

 Group size: 6

 Time: 10–15 minutes

 Resources: Whiteboard and pen

What to do

Explain to the students that they are going to take turns to think of different places to visit; for example 'I went to the palace/lake/zoo because…'. The other members of the group must each think of a different reason for going. Encourage the students to be creative in their choice of places and reasons for going. Ask the students to think about why this activity develops understanding. Encourage them to consider the thought processes involved in finding different reasons to support one statement, i.e. they must analyse the statement and be creative in their responses.

Extension

Write the following sentence on the whiteboard:

I went to the mountain because….

Invite the students to offer reasons and let the class vote to choose the most interesting answer.

UNDERSTANDING

Check the context

The students demonstrate understanding by substituting an incorrect word with one that is suitable for the given context.

 Group size: Pairs

 Time: 10–15 minutes

 Resources: For each pair, a copy of the photocopiable sheet *Check the context* (p. 129); pencils

What to do

Explain to the students that each sentence contains a word that does not fit into the context and therefore the sentence does not make sense. They must substitute the incorrect word for another, so that the sentence does make sense.

Extension

Ask each pair to make up five nonsense sentences of their own for another pair to change.

UNDERSTANDING

Why did?

This activity encourages the students to understand that people can respond in different ways to a given situation.

Group size: 6

Time: 10–15 minutes

Resources: Whiteboard and pen

What to do

Write the following sentences on the whiteboard.

- Why did Josh climb up an oak tree?
- Why did the tall man enter the cave?
- Why did Mrs Jones ring the police?
- Why did Sasha jump off a moving bus?
- Why did Ahmed run out of the house with a cat?
- Why did Dan hide the box behind a chair?

Explain to the students that they must each think of a reason to explain the actions of the people named. Encourage them to be creative with their reasons, which can be far-fetched. Discuss their reasons as a class and ask the students how they thought of their responses. For example, did they have a mental picture of the action? Would it help to have one?

Extension

Write the following sentence on the whiteboard:

- Why did the horse gallop down the road?

Explain that you are going to see which group can think of the most reasons in a given time.

UNDERSTANDING

Statement, question, answer

The students demonstrate that they understand statements.

 Group size: Pairs

 Time: 10–15 minutes

 Resources: None

What to do

Put the students into pairs. Explain that you will read them a statement and then ask a related question. They must think of an answer that does not directly repeat any of the statement, but still shows they have understood its meaning. For example:

S: The traffic lights were red. **Q:** Can Ahmed cross the road?
A: Yes, because the cars would be stopped.

1. **S:** It had been raining all night. **Q:** Can Stacey wear her flip-flops outside?
2. **S:** The dog had muddy paws. **Q:** Has Tyler taken the dog for a walk?
3. **S:** The petrol gauge was on empty. **Q:** Can Esme drive 100 miles in her car?
4. **S:** There was not a cloud in the sky. **Q:** Did Chen need to wear suntan lotion when she went out?
5. **S:** The empty plate was on the kitchen counter. **Q:** Had Jago eaten his dinner?

Discuss with the students how difficult/easy they found this activity. In particular, was it difficult to avoid using words in the statement? What helped them to create a suitable answer?

Extension

Ask the students to work out what the statement could be in the following examples:

Q: Had Monty the cat caught a bird? **A:** Yes, there was evidence on the floor of the kitchen.

Q: Had the horses escaped? **A:** Yes, the field was empty.

INTERPRETING

If a student can use the skill of interpretation, it means that they have developed confidence in their own abilities and judgements. These activities aim to enable students to look at stimulus material and offer their own ideas about it, showing higher-order skills such as synthesising and creating. The ability to interpret will also emphasise for a student that there are many different ways of viewing something and that their opinion is just as important as somebody else's.

INTERPRETING

What's in a dream?

The students interpret a dream to try and discover its meaning.

Group size: 2–3

Time: 10–15 minutes

Resources: For each group, a copy of the photocopiable sheet *What's in a dream?* (p. 130); paper and pencils

What to do

Discuss the topic of dreams with the students, asking them what they think the purpose of dreams could be. Explain that some people think that dreams can be interpreted and that all symbols in dreams have meaning; for example being in an alley signifies you have limited choices, being on a beach indicates that your future is calm and tranquil, black is unknown and mysterious, and cabbage is a warning of poverty. Ask the students to study the dream sequence and discuss its meaning. They can jot down their ideas on the paper. When the groups have completed this, they can compare their interpretations to see how similar or different they are and discuss why they made their choices.

Extension

Let each group make up a short dream sequence for another group to interpret. The groups can discuss how similar the interpretations are to the intended meanings.

INTERPRETING

Interpret the sign

The students discuss the meaning of signs that they are asked to interpret.

 Group size: Pairs

 Time: 10–15 minutes

 Resources: For each pair, a copy of the signs on the photocopiable sheet *Interpret the sign* (p. 131)

What to do

Explain to the students that they must study the signs and try to interpret their meaning.

Allow a set time for this and then call the students together to compare their interpretations, discussing the reasons for their choices. Ask them if they think that their interpretations would be globally accepted.

Extension

Ask the students to think of some signs that would be helpful in their school. They could be to supply information, regulate behaviour or generate emotions.

INTERPRETING

Mime requests

The students must mime a request for others to interpret.

 Group size: Whole class

 Time: 10–15 minutes

 Resources: Slips of paper on which requests are written (see below)

What to do

Write some requests on slips of paper, fold them in half and place them in a container. Some examples are: make me a cup of tea, read this book to me, switch on the light, help me put up this tent, make me a sandwich. Explain to the students that you are looking for volunteers to take a slip and mime the request for the others to guess. Tell them to think briefly through the appropriate actions. They can repeat the mime several times and answer questions to clarify their actions.

Extension

Put the students into pairs and ask them to work out a cooperative mime for the others to guess; for example making a bed, rowing a boat, sawing down a tree.

INTERPRETING

Why is the dog tied to the railings?

The students have to think collectively of all the possible interpretations of a scenario.

 Group size: Whole class

 Time: 5–10 minutes

 Resources: None

What to do

Read the following scenario to the students:

> The scene is a high street. A dog is tied to some railings in the street.

Ask the students to think collectively of as many different reasons as possible to explain this scenario. Discuss with the students what helped them to think of suitable reasons; for example knowledge of people's characters, a newspaper article, creative thinking.

Extension

Put the students into groups of three or four. Read the following scenario:

> The scene is a school playground. One solitary child is in the playground.

Ask each group to think of an explanation. Allow a few minutes for this then call the groups together to give their reasons.

Interpreting symbols

The students interpret symbols that represent different sports.

 Group size: 2–3

 Time: 15 minutes

 Resources: Paper and pencils; whiteboard and pen

What to do

Draw the following symbols on the whiteboard: a circle (a football), a rectangle with a line coming from the mid-point of a short side (a cricket bat) and a tick (a hockey stick). Explain that the symbols represent sports and ask the students which sport they think each symbol represents. Ask the students in their groups to think of and draw symbols for other different sports. The drawings must be very simple – remind them of the hockey stick. They then show their symbols to a different group and ask them to guess the sport involved. With their help, you can make a list of sports on the whiteboard to give them ideas if you wish.

Extension

Choose a couple of more obscure sports such as ice hockey, three-day eventing or synchronised swimming and ask the groups to think of appropriate symbols to represent each. Remind the students that the drawings must be as simple as possible.

INTERPRETING

Idioms

The students try and interpret the meaning of idioms.

 Group size: Whole class

 Time: 10 minutes

 Resources: None

What to do

Read out one idiom from the list below and explain to the students that it is a phrase that represents a meaning but is not literal. Tell them the meaning. Read out each idiom and ask the students to try and interpret the real meaning.

Pull your socks up.

Just what the doctor ordered.

Shaking in your boots.

Face the music.

In one ear and out the other.

In hot water.

In the dog house.

Don't lose your head.

Keep your eyes peeled.

Give me a hand.

Get off my case.

Get your skates on.

Bring home the bacon.

Making a mountain out of a molehill.

Your eyes are bigger than your stomach.

There's something fishy.

All fingers and thumbs.

Butterflies in your stomach.

Discuss with the students the purpose of idioms. How do they think they originated? Why are they less used today? Could they just have been a fashion at a certain time?

Extension

Ask the students to try and think up idioms for the following: feeling angry, something that is easy to do, talking too much.

INTERPRETING

Cockney rhyming slang

The students try to interpret rhyming slang to find its meaning.

 Group size: Whole class or pairs

 Time: 10–15 minutes

 Resources: None

What to do

Explain to the students that people from a certain part of London are referred to as cockneys. They have developed a language of rhyming slang; for example 'I went up the apples and pears (stairs), round the jolly horner (corner) and jumped into Uncle Ned (bed).

Ask the students to try and interpret the following rhyming slang:

I went into my Mickey Mouse (house).

I put on my new whistle and flute (suit).

I saw on the Dickory Dock (clock) that I was late.

The wind blew my Barnet Fair (hair) all over the place.

I took a butcher's hook (look) at the menu.

My plates of meat (feet) were killing me so I had to sit down.

Go and brush your Hampstead Heath (teeth).

You're in big Barney Rubble (trouble) – you haven't done your homework.

The man's trouble and strife (wife) was cross as he hadn't put out the recycling.

Can you answer the dog and bone (phone) because it keeps ringing.

The man ordered a glass of pig's ear (beer).

INTERPRETING

Ask the students why they think cockneys developed this slang. Was it to create a unique identity? Was it so that others would not understand what they were saying, or was it just for fun?

Extension

Ask the students to have a go at making up their own rhyming slang for the following: car, tea, chair, hand.

COLLATING

Collation signifies a movement towards greater independence of learning. It extends beyond simple retrieval as students begin to engage with stimulus material and work things out for themselves. It is a simple process but one which, when taught explicitly, will show the students that they can begin to make their own judgements on classroom material. The aim of these activities is to allow students to make something original from something taught.

When did it happen?

The students discuss the order of events so that they can place them on a timeline.

Group size: 10

Time: 15–20 minutes

Resources: The students bring in/research one news story each from the past year. They must know when it happened

What to do

Explain to the students that, through discussion, they are to place the news items in the correct time order of when they occurred.

Extension

Swap the group members around and ask them to repeat the process with different news items.

COLLATING

Categorise and collate

The students have to consider different aspects of objects to agree on a system of categorisation.

Group size: Whole class or groups of 10–12

Time: 20–30 minutes

Resources: Ask the students to bring in a small object from home. (Have a few suitable items for those students who forget.)

What to do

Sit in a large circle with the objects placed in front of the circle. Ask for suggestions on how to categorise the objects. It could be by function, size or what they are made of, and you can decide whether to limit the number of categories to four or five or to allow the students to determine how many there are. Once the objects have been placed into the agreed categories, the students involved can decide within their groups how to collate the items into a suitable sequence.

Extension

Call the students together with their objects and ask if there are any alternative categories that could have been used. How can they decide which is the best type of category? Is it the one that provides the most information?

COLLATING

Story sequence

The students must interpret a set of pictures in order to collate them successfully.

Group size: 4

Time: 15–20 minutes

Resources: A copy of the comic strips on the photocopiable sheet *Story sequence* (p. 132) cut into individual boxes. This activity is designed for a class of 20. If you have more students, you will need to photocopy the page twice and use each sequence more than once

What to do

Give each member of the group two of the boxes from one comic strip in a random order, but give each group one incorrect box from a different strip. Ask the students to decide what is happening in the strip and put the boxes into the correct order. When they discover that one of their boxes does not fit, ask them to find their correct box among the other groups.

Variation

Keeping one box from each strip, place the remaining boxes randomly on various tables around the room. Give each group one box and ask them to find the remaining seven and then put them into the correct sequence.

COLLATING

Oldest to youngest

Whole group cooperation is required in this activity, as the students put themselves into the correct age order.

 Group size: Whole class

 Time: 10–15 minutes

 Resources: None

What to do

Ask the students to put themselves into the correct age order, starting with the oldest. Time how long this takes.

Extension

Ask the students to put themselves in the correct order for shoe size, starting with the smallest. Time them to see if they can complete this in a quicker time than they did for the ages activity.

Rules of the school

The students consider the importance of different rules.

 Group size: 4–5

 Time: 20+ minutes

 Resources: Paper and pencils

What to do

Explain to the students that they are going to think of 20 rules for an imaginary school within their group. These can be serious, such as no swearing, or less serious, such as boys should wear black shoes. When they have completed this, the groups discuss their rules and put them in order of importance for the smooth running of a school. Each group reads out their list of rules to compare and contrast with the other groups. The students can discuss the similarities and differences.

Variation

Collect and write onto cards enough school rules for the students to have one each. Ask the whole class to discuss and decide on the order of the rules, starting with the most important. The students arrange themselves in the agreed order. If there is disagreement, take a vote by a show of hands.

COLLATING

Colours of the rainbow

The students collate lists of items into a set order.

 Group size: 2–3

 Time: 10 minutes

 Resources: Paper and pencils; whiteboard and pen

What to do

Write the following lists on the whiteboard and ask the students to collate them into the order given.

1. Indigo, yellow, blue, red, violet, green, orange. The order of the colours of the rainbow.

2. Lunch, supper, elevenses, dinner, breakfast, afternoon snack, tea. The order of meals throughout the day.

3. Valentine's Day, Bonfire Night, Easter, Christmas Day, Halloween, May Day, New Year's Eve. The order of festivities throughout the year.

4. Manchester, Penzance, John O'Groats, Birmingham, Land's End, Newcastle, London. The order of places north to south.

Extension

Write the place names on the whiteboard in the correct order. Ask for volunteers to slot other place names into the order in the correct place. You may want to have an atlas handy to check the suggestions.

COLLATING

Which word comes first?

The students collate lists of words into the correct order and against the clock.

Group size: 3–4

Time: 10 minutes

Resources: Paper and pencils

What to do

Explain to the students that you will read or write up, whichever you prefer, a list of seven words. They are to put them into the correct dictionary order as quickly as possible. Time how long it takes for the first group to finish, then ask them to read out their words. If they are correct, continue with another list. Tell the students they must try to beat the previous time set, as this is the current record.

1. Public, lemon, private, melon, privet, lime, practice
2. Next, natural, neat, notice, nut, nice, never
3. Ring, rice, rip, rich, ripe, rinse, river

Extension

Ask the groups each to think of seven words, without using a dictionary, and write them out in the correct alphabetical order.

REFINING

When a student refines something, they have to make it more fine, subtle or precise. It is a skill that requires total engagement of the student as they are changing the state of something, rather than swapping something around or using simple retrieval. The aim of these activities is to allow students to make a personal judgement about material and begin to develop independence from basic knowledge retention towards original thought.

Short and sweet

The students must focus on the important elements of a story.

 Group size: Pairs

 Time: 20–30 minutes

 Resources: A selection of stories cut from newspapers (choose ones with a strong or dramatic storyline and don't include the headlines); a newspaper account of the sinking of the *Titanic* (you can download one from the internet); paper and pencils

What to do

Read the account of the sinking of the *Titanic* to the students. Explain that if you wanted to describe this in the shortest possible way you could write 'Iceberg sinks ship'. Tell the students that they are going to look at the news stories and then try and describe them in the shortest possible way that conveys the main action in the stories. The students work through as many of the stories as they can in the given time. Call the students together to compare their sentences.

Variation

Give each pair the same story and compare their sentences. Take a vote on the sentence that they think best conveys the action in the shortest way.

REFINING

Smiley faces

The students consider various factors that might influence a smile in their quest to find the 'happiest' image.

 Group size: 3–4

 Time: 10–15 minutes

 Resources: You need to find 15–20 magazine photos of people smiling and laughing. Try and find some where the smile appears false or is barely a smirk; whiteboard

What to do

Attach the photos of the faces that you have collected to a whiteboard. Number each photo. Ask the groups to study the photos and then discuss and choose the three that they consider to be the happiest. Ask them to give reasons for their choices. Compare the choices of the groups to see how similar they are and discuss the reasons for any differences.

Variation

Although it might be more difficult to access material, you could repeat this activity with disgruntled/angry faces.

The sum total

The students refine complicated sums by simplifying the processes.

Group size: 3–4

Time: 15 minutes

Resources: Whiteboard and pen; paper and pencils; calculators

What to do

Write out the following sums on a whiteboard:

12 × 2 + 6 – 14 + 7 + 25 – 19 × 3 = 87

45 ÷ 5 × 3 + 36 – 28 + 16 + 9 – 20 × 4 = 160

Put the students into groups of three or four with mixed ability in mathematics, so that those with low attainment are not daunted by this activity. Ask the students to simplify the sums, first to five steps, then four, then three, then two, all with the same answer.

Extension

Ask each group to make up a sum using their calculators and get the groups to repeat the above process.

REFINING

Wishes

The students refine a selection of suggestions into one that best incorporates all the others.

 Group size: 5–6

 Time: 15–20 minutes

 Resources: Paper and pencils; whiteboard and pen

What to do

Ask the students, within their groups, each to think of a way of improving school dinners and make a note of them. When they have completed this they read through the list and think of a way of incorporating all or most of the suggestions into one sentence. Let each group state their suggestion and, if there are differences, write them up and work as a whole class to refine them into one overall suggestion.

Variation

Ask the students, within their groups, to think of a reason why school uniforms are a good idea and then refine these into one overall reason.

REFINING

Too much talk

The students refine a speech in order to present just the relevant information.

 Group size: 3–4

 Time: 20+ minutes

 Resources: Paper and pencils

What to do

Explain to the students that you are going to read a speech to them (see below) and that the person talking rather likes the sound of their own voice and takes a long time to impart information that could be said in one sentence. The students listen carefully and then refine the speech into one sentence that contains the relevant information. They write the sentence down and the groups take turns to read theirs out. You may need to read the extract two or three times.

'Hi Josh, I thought that we might meet on Saturday because I know you're not playing football and I've got a free afternoon as my mum and dad are out for the day so I don't have to go anywhere with them. We could meet outside the railway station. I think that's probably the best place, although sometimes it's quite crowded there, but it's easy to get to and if someone is late it's quite nice to stand there and watch all the people coming and going – you never know who you will see or maybe something exciting might happen right in front of your eyes. Anyway, you could walk there in 15 minutes or you might want to catch the number 39 bus. I think the number 25 stops there as well. I'll probably catch the 14 by the post office near my house. I thought that we could meet at three as that is a good time for me, so I hope that it won't be too early for you if you were doing something in the morning or too late for you if you had planned to go out later on. It seemed like an ideal time to me, you know, bang in the middle of the afternoon. Regan will be with me. I think he's a friend of yours too, or at least someone you don't mind, although I know that he can be a bit self-

REFINING

> obsessed at times. Do you remember the time he went on for ages about his score on the game? I think he was jabbering on for ten minutes or was it 15? Anyway, I know that it was a long time because I had lost the will to live. He's not that bad, though, and we could go to Archie's Café, or Greet and Eat or the Garden Café. I like to have a latte, but I think you prefer a cold drink, so you could have a cola or fruit juice and Regan can choose. They do a nice hot chocolate at Archie's so that might be the best place, although the Garden Café has the best views overlooking the river. There again, it might be too cold to go there at this time of the year. Anyway, what do you think?'

This could be simplified to 'Hi Josh, would you like to meet me and Regan on Saturday at three o'clock outside the railway station for a drink?'

Extension

Ask the groups to think of something they want to say in a speech. They pad it out with as much superfluous material as they can and write it down. A member from each group reads out the speech and the other groups decide on a sentence that incorporates the important information.

Desert island list

The students refine a list into six essential items.

 Group size: Individual or pairs

 Time: 5–10 minutes

 Resources: Paper and pencils; whiteboard and pen

What to do

Write the following list on the whiteboard:

Sun cream, torch, fishing net, bedroll, knife, spoon, tent, mallet, blanket, radio, mosquito net, matches, solar-powered fridge, bucket, cooking pot, sun hat, insect repellent, airtight container, book, paper and pencils, plastic bottle.

Explain to the students that they must decide on the six items that they would consider most essential to take to a desert island. Record the most popular items by putting a tick or a dot next to each item on the whiteboard. What were the most popular items?

Extension

Take a class vote on each item from this list to decide on the six items considered most essential. (Remind the students that they can only choose six.)

REFINING

Refine and unrefine

The students look at both sides of the coin in this activity in which they are asked to both refine sentences and make them less refined.

 Group size: 3–4

 Time: 15–20 minutes

 Resources: Paper and pencils; whiteboard and pen

What to do

Read the following sentence to the students: 'Eh by gum, I think the devil himself would freeze in hell today' and explain that put simply it means 'It's very cold.' Conversely, the sentence, 'She is a good actress' could be indicated by saying, 'Well, I'll tell you what, when she came on stage it was as if an extra bright bulb had been switched on.'

Ask the groups to think of a simple statement and 'unrefine' it by adding a lot of superfluous words and expressions. They swap this sentence with another group and each has to try and refine it back to its original sentence.

Extension

Ask the groups to write out a sentence using colloquialisms rather than plain English. Choose two and write them on the whiteboard for the other groups to refine.

INFERRING

The ability to infer means that students are able to judge or conclude something from stimulus material, but not through explicit teaching. These activities aim to allow students to develop subtly within their learning and to think about what is implied, rather than what is stated.

INFERRING

Where am I?

The students use their experience to pick out the key elements of phrases that give clues as to their settings.

 Group: Individual

 Time: 15–20 minutes

 Resources: Paper and pencils

What to do

Explain to the students that you are going to read out some phrases that could be spoken by people in certain places. Tell the students to write 1–12 on their paper. Ask the students to guess the place from the clues given in each phrase and write it against the appropriate number.

1. 'Two tickets for screen one, please.' (*Cinema*)
2. 'Mr Jones to consulting room one, please.' (*Doctor's surgery/hospital*)
3. 'A farmhouse loaf and three doughnuts, please.' (*Bakery/supermarket*)
4. 'I'll have the Beef Wellington with French fries, please.' (*Restaurant*)
5. 'Right sir, you need to press your finger onto the ink-pad and then place it onto the card.' (*Police station*)
6. 'I've come to collect the package that wouldn't fit through my letter box.' (*Post office*)
7. 'Please don't throw any confetti until you get outside.' (*Church/registry office*)
8. 'Did you want the ends trimmed?' (*Hairdressing salon*)
9. 'The coins in that display case are over a thousand years old.' (*Museum*)
10. 'Three balls to get a coconut.' (*Funfair*)

INFERRING

11. 'See if you can blow them out in one go and make a wish.' (*Birthday party*)
12. 'This model has a lever on the side so that you can recline it and put your feet up.' (*Furniture shop*)

Extension

Put the students into pairs and ask them to think of a different place or situation with an appropriate phrase.

INFERRING

Who and what?

The students have to infer certain facts from conversations.

 Group size: 2–3

 Time: 10–15 minutes

 Resources: None

What to do

Put the students into pairs or groups of three. Read the following short conversations to them and ask them to deduce who is speaking and what is happening.

1. **A:** 'I'm sorry but this document is out of date.'

   B: 'What does that mean?'

   A: 'You won't be allowed on board.' (*Passenger trying to board a plane/boat with an out-of-date passport, and an official*)

2. **A:** 'You'll need to close them all if I'm going to wash them.'

   B: 'Have you got a ladder to reach the top ones?'

   A: 'Yes, there's one on my van.' (*Window cleaner and client*)

3. **A:** 'Everyone will be there and seated when we arrive. How are you feeling?'

   B: 'Very nervous, I'm worried I'll trip over the hem of my dress. I'm glad I've got you to walk in with so I can hold onto your arm.'

   A: 'Well, you look very beautiful behind your veil, and the flowers look and smell gorgeous.' (*Bride and father travelling to her wedding*)

78

INFERRING

4. **A:** 'He's looking in good form and raring to go. What should I do?'

   B: 'Yes, he's in peak condition and he likes this soft ground. Hold him steady for the first half, then push him on.' (*Jockey and trainer discussing a horse and race tactics*)

5. **A:** 'But I'm her closest living relative.'

   B: 'That may be so, but according to this, everything goes to the cats' home.' (*Solicitor and deceased person's relative at the reading of a will*)

Extension

Let each group devise a similar short script that infers, rather than states explicitly, what is happening.

INFERRING

What can you deduce?

The students are asked to infer certain facts from the text, without them being explicitly stated.

Group size: Individual

Time: 10–15 minutes

Resources: For each student, a copy of the passage and questions on the photocopiable sheet *What can you deduce?* (p. 133); pencils

What to do

Give the students each a copy of the passage and questions and ask them to read through the text and answer the questions underneath. Discuss with them how they knew the answers when they were not given explicitly, i.e. they used clues in the passage to deduce the correct answers.

Variation

For more able students, you could read the passage to them and ask the questions. With each answer volunteered, ask what specific clue helped them to deduce the answer.

INFERRING

Faces

The students must infer the correct emotion from the faces displayed.

Group size: 6

Time: 15–20 minutes

Resources: A set of cards with a different emotion written on each one; for example happy, sad, excited, angry, bored, lonely, frightened, worried

What to do

Put the class into groups of six. Place the emotions cards face down on a surface. Ask each group to stand in a line, one behind the other and all facing the same way. Ask the last person in each line to collect an emotions card. They must not show the card to the other members of their group or tell them what is written on their card. The players resume their places at the back of the line. They tap the player directly in front of them on the shoulder to request that they turn round. The last player in the line then puts on an appropriate expression to match the emotion on their card. The second from last player taps the person directly in front of them to turn round and repeats the expression, and so on down the line. The player at the front of the line guesses the emotion. If incorrect, the other players can have a turn at guessing.

Extension

This activity can be repeated with an added keyword for each emotion. The last player in the line thinks of a situation linked to the keyword and emotion and the other players try to guess the situation. For example, if the emotion was angry and the keyword was bicycle the situation might be a puncture while out cycling. If the emotion was frightened and the keyword was house, the situation might be alone in a haunted house.

INFERRING

What's happened?

The students try and infer what has happened prior to the scenes depicted in a set of illustrations.

 Group size: 2–3

 Time: 10–15 minutes

 Resources: For each pair/group, a set of the illustrations from the photocopiable sheet *What's happened?* (p. 134)

What to do

Give each pair/group a set of the illustrations and ask them to infer what is happening and why. For example, in the first illustration people may be hiding to jump out and surprise the person entering; it could be a game of hide-and-seek or a surprise birthday party. When the students have made their decisions, ask the groups to discuss each picture in turn to compare how similar or different their interpretations were. Encourage the students to describe what helped them to reach their decisions.

Extension

Choose one of the illustrations and list all the visual clues from each group. Discuss how we 'read' visual clues in life, such as tone of voice, facial expression and body language, to help us understand situations.

INFERRING

What is going on?

The students infer what is happening from studying the poses taken up by each group.

 Group size: 6

 Time: 20+ minutes

 Resources: A slip of paper for each group on which is written one of the scenarios below

What to do

Give each group one of the scenarios. They are to discuss their scenarios in whispers and then take up still poses in a tableau that depicts what is happening in their scenario.

1. A player has scored a goal in a game of football. The goal-keeper is on the ground. Two players look sad/angry while two members of the opposing team and the goal scorer look jubilant.
2. A tug-of-war with two opposing teams.
3. Three teams are in a relay race about to hand over the baton.
4. A group is waiting for a person who is just about to enter a surprise birthday party.
5. Two people are playing tennis. There are three spectators all looking the same way and one is an umpire watching the action.
6. Spectators are watching a high-wire artist. One is pointing up, one is looking happily excited, one is looking terrified and one has covered their eyes. The remaining two are a mother and her child, who has buried her head against her mother.

Each group, in turn, takes up their poses for the others to guess what is happening.

Extension

Ask for volunteers to mime an action for the others to guess.

INFERRING

Who would wear that?

The students infer people's professions from a description of their clothing.

 Group size: 2–3

 Time: 5–10 minutes

 Resources: Paper and pencils

What to do

Read out the following descriptions of outfits. After each outfit, ask the students to write down who they think would wear such clothes.

1. A thick white suit, white boots, long, thick white gloves, a helmet with a glass face panel. (*Astronaut*)

2. A hard hat with a peak, tight white trousers, a coloured and patterned silk top, long black boots. (*Jockey*)

3. A white apron and a tall white hat. (*Chef*)

4. A white net skirt, a sequinned top, a feather headdress, satin shoes tied with ribbons. (*Ballerina*)

5. A long green overall, a green face mask, a green head square, latex gloves. (*Surgeon*)

6. A waterproof coat, a waterproof hat, wellington boots. (*Farmer/gardener*)

Extension

Ask each pair/group to think of someone in a specific profession and describe their clothes for the others to guess.

ANALYSING

The ability to analyse means to examine material carefully and separate it into its constituent parts or elements, while at the same time making personal judgements regarding findings. These activities aim to focus students on stimulus material and to aid concentration.

ANALYSING

Guess what I am

The students analyse a set of descriptions in order to guess what job is involved in each case.

 Group size: 2–3

 Time: 10–15 minutes

 Resources: Paper and pencils

What to do

Explain to the students that you will read out different extracts. In each case, they must try to work out the occupation of the speaker.

1. 'I spend a lot of time in my van, but of course I get to stop on every road. Sometimes, especially if it's a hot day, there's quite a queue waiting for me. Everyone knows when I'm around as they hear my jingle.' (*Ice cream salesman*)

2. 'It's very quiet where I work, although sometimes it's quite full with people at every table. I push my trolley up and down the aisles, putting the returns back on the shelves for the next borrower. I like the children's section best – so many lovely illustrations.' (*Librarian*)

3. 'It's not really very wobbly considering that we travel at speeds of up to 120 miles per hour. It takes me about 15 to 20 minutes to work my way from one end to the other, depending on how full we are. If I meet the lady selling drinks and snacks on the way, it's a tight squeeze to get past.' (*Train conductor*)

4. 'I've always been fast, and lifting weights has given me upper body strength. I'm six feet, five inches tall so have a good reach and cover the court well. I travel to tournaments all over the world and sometimes play in doubles as well.' (*Tennis player*)

5. 'Oh the noise is unbelievable when they're all in here. Some of them are so fussy, they don't like this and they don't like that – goodness knows what they eat at home. Others are alright, though, and come up for seconds. It's a relief when the bell goes and I can get some peace and quiet.' (*School dinner supervisor*)

Extension

Ask each group to make up a similar description of a person's job for the others to guess.

ANALYSING

The sum of many parts

The students are asked to study and analyse component parts to try and work out the object.

 Group size: Pairs

 Time: 10–15 minutes

 Resources: A set of numbered cards on which you have glued the images as instructed below; paper and pencils

What to do

Collect photographs of objects from magazines and cut each image into several parts. Glue the component parts for each image onto a piece of card in a random order. Number each card. You will need a sufficient number of objects for one per pair and a few spare. Explain to the students that they must analyse the photographs of the component parts and guess the object that they make up. They write the number of the card onto their paper and the name of the object alongside it. They then take a different card and repeat the process.

Extension

Find a large photograph of an active scene, such as people skiing or having a picnic. Cover the photograph with a sheet of paper and make a few small holes in the paper that allow a glimpse of the scene underneath. Ask the students to analyse what they can see in order to guess the scene.

ANALYSING

Study the picture

The students study a busy picture in order to answer questions.

 Group size: Individual or pairs

 Time: 20 minutes

 Resources: For each student/pair, a copy of the busy picture and questions on the photocopiable sheets *Study the picture* (pp. 135–136); pencils

What to do

The students study and analyse the picture in order to answer the questions.

Extension

The students turn over their pictures and answer the following questions that you read to them one at a time.

1. What is the name on the ice cream van?
2. What is studying the fish?
3. What large vehicle is by the park entrance?
4. What can jump high?
5. What's happened to the cricketers?

ANALYSING

Riddles

The students analyse sentences for clues to help them identify objects.

 Group size: Pairs

 Time: 10–15 minutes

 Resources: Paper and pencils

What to do

Read the following sentences out slowly two or three times and ask the students to guess what you are talking about. If they find this activity difficult, stop after each sentence to discuss what it could mean. Examples are given in the first two riddles.

- I like the moon but not the sun (*nocturnal*). I live on high but search down low (*something that lives in trees but looks on the ground for food*). I'm soft, downy and cuddly but also sharp, pointy and scratchy (*soft plumage and sharp talons and claws*). I'm a real hoot. What am I? (*An owl*)

- I'm quiet when switched off, but noisy when switched on (*a machine*). You can push me or pull me around (*a machine that can be carried about*). The more I clean the dirtier I get. What am I? (*A vacuum cleaner*)

- I run, but I do not walk. I'm fresh at the start and salty at the end. I can split off in different directions but I always end up in the same place. What am I? (*A river*)

- I am a line with no beginning and no end. I have no corners or edges and I keep going forever. I never stop. What am I? (*A circle*)

- I have a face and hands, but no arms or legs. I can let you know when you need to get up and you can look at me if you want to know if lunch is ready. I can sit on a table by your bed or be as tall as a grandfather in the hall. What am I? (*A clock*)

ANALYSING

Extension

If the students have been able to guess these quite easily, try them with the trickier riddles below.

- You look at me and then you look at you. I show you what you want to see. I am made of glass but you can't see through me. What am I? (*A mirror*)
- I can fit on one fingertip when young, but I will dwarf you when I'm fully grown. When it's cold I stand naked but when it's warm I am fully clothed. I am firmly grounded, although I may have my head in the clouds. I need no home, but am home to many. What am I? (*A tree*)

ANALYSING

Who likes what?

The students analyse a chart of different people's likes and dislikes to determine who ordered which meal.

 Groups: Pairs

 Time: 10–15 minutes

 Resources: For each pair, a copy of the photocopiable sheet *Who likes what?* (p. 137)

What to do

Give each pair a copy of the chart of likes and dislikes and ask the following questions.

1. Who ordered chips, chicken, beans and juice? (*Danny*)
2. Who ordered fish, coleslaw, salad and cola? (*Ben*)
3. Who ordered chicken, salad, beans and a milkshake? (*Frazer*)
4. Who ordered chips, burger, beans and a smoothie? (*Enrique*)

Extension

Make a similar chart for the class. Ask each student to choose someone and write down a meal they might order. Then get them to ask another student to try and identify the person they have chosen. (Explain that there might be more than one person who fits.)

ANALYSING

Sort them out

The students analyse jumbled up paragraphs to sort them out correctly.

 Group size: Pairs

 Time: 10 minutes

 Resources: For each pair, a copy of the photocopiable sheet *Sort them out* (p. 138); paper and pencils

What to do

Give each pair of students a copy of the photocopied sheet and ask them to sort the sentences out and group them into the correct paragraphs. Ask the students what helped them to work this out.

Extension

Read the following paragraph to the students two or three times and ask them to identify and write down all the occupations that are referred to.

> 'I get up really early to do the milking (*farmer*) and finish my round by early afternoon when I take the packets that wouldn't fit through the door back to the central office (*postman*). I give out tablets to the patients two or three times a day (*nurse*) and sweep the floors and empty the bins when everyone has gone home (*cleaner*). I don't like having to do maths on a Friday afternoon when all they want to do is go home (*teacher*), but I'm riding at Kempton and hope the going is soft as he will jump better (*jockey*). Sometimes I break a string during a rally (*tennis player*) and at other times I make a squeaky noise when I draw the bow across the strings (*violin player*). It's a long way down from the high board and I have to enter perfectly so that I don't make a splash (*diver*). They prefer bolognese to stew and so more will come up for seconds when that is on (*school dinner supervisor*).

ANALYSING

Spot the difference

The students analyse two drawings to find the differences between them.

 Group size: Individual

 Time: 10–15 minutes

 Resources: For each student, a copy of the photocopiable sheets *Spot the difference* (pp. 140–141)

What to do

Hand out the drawings and ask the students to mark the differences on one of the drawings. Allow a set time and then ask them to count how many they have found. Let the student with the most differences describe the ones they have found. Ask if anyone has discovered others and, if so, let them give details.

Variation

Give out the drawings and ask the first student to discover 20 differences to raise their hand.

EVALUATING

When evaluating, students offer original ideas regarding the success of stimulus material in certain requisite criteria, demonstrating their understanding of the criteria given. Original evaluation illustrates complete engagement and synthesis of the subject matter. The aim of these activities is to encourage students to display certainty and confidence in their own judgements, valuing their own opinions as much as any others.

EVALUATING

Likes/dislikes

This activity introduces the concept of evaluation as the students appreciate that people have different personal tastes.

 Group size: Whole class and pairs

 Time: 10–15 minutes

 Resources: None

What to do

Divide the room into three zones; for example right-hand side for likes, left-hand side for dislikes and centre for neither. Explain to the students that you will call out categories and they are to choose which area to stand in according to their responses. The centre is for students who don't have strong feelings either way. Tell the students that you will give the signal for them to move, but before this they are to tell someone standing close to them whether they think the likes or dislikes will score the highest. After the students have moved, ask if anyone was surprised by the result and why. Examples of categories could be dogs, Marmite, a TV show, swimming, picnics.

Extension

Put the students into pairs with a partner with whom they would not normally spend time. Call out different categories and each time ask the students to guess their partner's response before they make it.

EVALUATING

The best advert

The students evaluate the adverts to decide which is best in terms of promoting a product and why.

 Group size: 3–4

 Time: 10–15 minutes

 Resources: Collect a set of different adverts from magazines about one particular product; for example shampoo, cars, holidays

What to do

Ask the students to look at and compare the selection of adverts. They should discuss the properties of each advert and decide which they consider promotes the product well and why.

Extension

Ask the groups to discuss their favourite TV adverts and agree on one that they all consider sells the product well. Ask the students to give reasons for their choices about what makes their chosen advert so appealing.

EVALUATING

What's the most important?

The students are asked to evaluate aspects of life and place them in order of importance.

 Group size: 4–6

 Time: 15 minutes

 Resources: Paper and pencils; whiteboard and pen

What to do

Write the following list on the whiteboard:

> Health, money, fitness, freedom of speech, family, hobbies, friends, home

Ask the groups to discuss the categories and then place them in order of importance in their lives. When the groups have all completed this, call them together to discuss their choices.

Extension

Take a whole-class vote on the students' top three categories in order of importance. Ask the students how many were surprised at the results and why.

EVALUATING

I would rather

The students are asked to evaluate statements and either agree or disagree with the sentiment.

Group size: 6

Time: 10–15 minutes

Resources: For each group, a set of statements from the photocopiable sheet *I would rather* (p. 142), cut up and put into a container

What to do

The students take turns to pick a statement out of the container and read it to the rest of the group. The students each say whether they agree or disagree with each statement and give a reason for their response.

Extension

Each student thinks up a statement of their own to say to the group. The rest of the group say whether they agree or disagree with each statement.

EVALUATING

The best present

The students evaluate 'gifts' to decide which is the most desirable.

Group size: 6

Time: 10–15 minutes

Resources: Whiteboard and pen

What to do

You can decide whether or not to put the students into single-sex groups for this activity. Without discussion, each student thinks of a present they would give to someone up to the value of £500. When all the members of the group have thought of their presents, they each state what they have chosen and what makes it so desirable. The group then votes on the best present. It may take several votes if numbers are tied.

Extension

Each group states their choice of present and these are written on the whiteboard for a whole-class vote.

EVALUATING

The best headteacher

The students analyse the qualities needed to be a headteacher.

Group size: 4

Time: 15 minutes

Resources: Whiteboard and pen

What to do

Make a list on the whiteboard of people with leadership qualities, such as the Queen, Lord Sugar, Simon Cowell, Prince Charles, Karren Brady. Ask the groups to discuss who from the list would make the best headteacher and why. Let each group explain their choice and then take a class vote.

Extension

Ask the students to make a list of all the qualities they would wish to see in a headteacher if they were going to advertise for one.

EVALUATING

Gobbledegook

The students evaluate sounds and combinations of words to produce interesting nonsense words.

 Group size: 2–3

 Time: 15 minutes

 Resources: Paper and pencils; a copy of Lewis Carroll's poem *Jabberwocky*

What to do

Read the students some lines from Lewis Carroll's *Jabberwocky*, explaining that it is a nonsense poem. The words can be combinations of other words or just made up. (Wikipedia has a good explanation of the poem.) So, for example, if you wanted to describe something that was sleek and fast you might describe it as 'slast' or 'fleek'. You might decide to make up a new word instead that you think sounds descriptive, such as 'thwooshy'. Ask the students to combine words or make up new words to describe the following:

- Hot and spicy
- A drip on the end of a nose
- A big, clumpy shoe
- A high-pitched screech
- A flat tyre
- A fierce dog.

Extension

Make a list of the words for the fierce dog and take a class vote on which the students think best portrays the meaning.

INVESTIGATING

To investigate means to examine, study or inquire into systematically. These activities aim to encourage students to search out and examine the particulars of something in an attempt to learn the hidden or complex facts. This is a skill that students will need to achieve cross-curricular success. Many homework tasks are investigative and research-based, and students who develop confidence in their ability to discover information independently, both at school and at home, will develop self-reliance and greater control of their own learning.

INVESTIGATING

Who walked on my flowerbed?

The students take turns to investigate footprints and discover the 'culprit' through a process of questioning, looking and elimination.

Group size: Whole class

Time: 20 minutes

Resources: Black sugar paper and chalk

What to do

Choose two students to leave the room. Make a footprint from one of the remaining students by rubbing chalk over the sole of their shoe and printing this onto the black paper. Make sure that the student cleans the chalk thoroughly from the sole of their shoe afterwards, to leave no visible trace. Call the two students back into the room and show them the footprint, saying, 'This person has walked on my flowerbed. Can you find out who it is?' The students examine the footprint and by noting the size, shape and pattern of the tread, they try and work out who it belongs to. They can ask to see different shoes to compare them with the print. Repeat the process with different students.

Variation

Ask for 12 volunteers to stand in an 'identity parade'. Tell the other students to study their appearances carefully. Ask the 12 to go outside the door with an adult and for two of them to exchange an item of visible clothing. They return to the room and the other students try to guess what has been changed.

Legends

The students investigate legends to discover facts about them and formulate arguments over whether they are real or not.

 Group size: 4

 Time: 30+ minutes

 Resources: The internet; library; paper and pencils

What to do

Put the students into groups of four and give each group a legend, such as the Loch Ness Monster, Bigfoot, the Beast of Bodmin Moor, vampires, werewolves. Explain that two of the group must look for facts to support the argument that the legend is real, while the other pair looks for facts to support the argument that the legend is just a myth and doesn't exist. When the groups have investigated their legends, call the class together and let each pair present their facts.

Extension

Choose one of the legends for a whole-class discussion and take a vote on whether or not the students believe it exists.

INVESTIGATING

Find the facts

The students investigate different questions to discover the facts behind them.

 Group size: Pairs

 Time: 30+ minutes

 Resources: The internet; library; paper and pencils

What to do

Ask the students to think of a question that they would like to investigate in their pairs, such as 'Why is the sun hot?', 'Why do we cry?', 'Where is the coldest place on Earth?' Allow them a set time to use the internet or the library to gather as many facts as possible. Let each pair present their investigations to the rest of the class.

Extension

Set a whole-class question and give the students a week to see who can discover the most facts.

What's the story?

The students take turns to investigate through questioning, in order to discover the facts of a story.

Group size: 6

Time: 20+ minutes

Resources: Paper and pencils; whiteboard and pen

What to do

Explain to the students that they are going to take turns to be journalists. Divide the groups into pairs and give each pair one of these storylines:

- A lady in a large store has her handbag stolen.
- A horse gets loose and gallops through a busy event.
- A hoard of treasure is discovered in a field.

Allow the pairs five minutes to study their storylines away from other members of the group. The pairs can embellish the stories by adding details of their own, such as the colour of clothes, hairstyles or the time of the event. They then take turns to be journalists and question another pair about their event to establish as many facts as they can. If they ask a question that does not have a prepared answer, the students must make up an answer on the spot. The pair asking the questions numbers and writes down each fact that they have learnt. Call the students together to find out which pair discovered the greatest number of facts.

Extension

Write the following sentence on the whiteboard:

Crowds wait to see Saphina as she arrives at the airport.

Give the pairs five minutes to think of as many fact-finding questions as they can. Find out which pair has the most questions and write them on the whiteboard. Ask if any other pairs have different questions to add.

INVESTIGATING

All boys like football

The students investigate statements to find out whether or not they are true.

 Group size: 2–3

 Time: 20 minutes

 Resources: Paper and pencils

What to do

Give each pair a statement from the list below and ask them to canvass the other students for their responses. They must phrase their questions correctly in order to get the right information. For example, for the statement 'Boys like football' they must ask the boys only, 'Do you like football?' Once everyone has completed this, the students present their findings. They can either do this by numbering how many agreed or disagreed with the statement or by giving percentages.

- Boys like football.
- Girls like the colour pink.
- Everyone likes ice cream.
- People prefer a hot sunny day to a cold wintry day.
- Everyone is scared of spiders.
- Everyone thinks slugs are worse than worms.
- Girls are scared of mice.
- Boys like playing computer/Xbox/PlayStation games.
- Everyone hates homework.
- Nobody likes the taste of Brussels sprouts.
- Everyone loves chocolate.
- All girls used to play with Barbie dolls.
- All boys used to have scooters.

Extension

Compare the results for each statement to see which statement is closest to the truth.

INVESTIGATING

Investigative questions

The students work in groups to think of good investigative questions that will provide the most information.

 Group size: 3–4

 Time: 15–20 minutes

 Resources: Paper and pencils

What to do

Choose a topic such as the solar system or endangered species. Ask the groups to think of five questions related to the topic. They must consider which questions will provide the most information about the topic. Call the groups together to reveal their questions and ask them what prompted their choices.

Extension

Take a class vote to discover the five best questions.

INVESTIGATING

Which country?

The students investigate countries to find five features that are representative.

 Group size: 2–3

 Time: 30 minutes

 Resources: The internet; paper and pencils

What to do

Give each group a different country to investigate. Explain that they must try and find five items relating to the country that they think are representative. For example, if they are researching France they might decide on: garlic, the Eiffel Tower, berets, sunflowers and frogs' legs. Some suggested countries are: Italy, Mexico, Australia, China, Japan, India, Canada, America, Russia.

Ask the groups to write the name of the country and list the five items underneath. Put all the slips of paper into a container and pull one out at random. Read out the five items and ask the students to guess the country. The students who investigated and wrote the items must keep quiet.

Extension

Prepare lists for two countries not mentioned prior to the lesson and read them out, inviting the students to guess the identity.

EXPLORING

Exploring in educational terms means to look into closely, to scrutinise or examine. Students are able to look at taught material and make independent judgements on it, such as exploring possibilities for improvement. These activities aim to help students to understand that there may be deeper meanings to certain things, and to look into the component parts, focusing on detail as well as the bigger picture.

EXPLORING

Design a set

The students explore the features that would best create the atmosphere and depict the scene for a given stage play.

 Group size: 3–4

 Time: 20 minutes

 Resources: Paper and pencils; whiteboard and pen

What to do

Explain to the students that they are going to design a suitable set for a given play. They must consider the backdrop and props that would evoke a suitable atmosphere and set the best scene, and make a list of these or write some sentences about them. You can either write a choice of scenarios on the whiteboard and allow the students to choose an option, or ask the groups to complete the same task and compare the results. Some ideas for plays are:

- Astronauts have landed on a distant planet.
- A ghost story.
- People have travelled back to prehistoric times.

Ask each group to explain their choices to the other groups.

Extension

Ask the class to consider what sort of effects are used in films to create a creepy and suspense-filled atmosphere; for example shadows, windows banging, owls hooting and branches scratching a window.

EXPLORING

What's in a name?

The students explore the use of names to depict the different characters of people.

 Groups: Pairs

 Time: 15–20 minutes

 Resources: Paper and pencils

What to do

Explain to the students that authors have sometimes used names specifically to give the reader an impression of the characters of people in their books. For example, Charles Dickens had characters with names such as Mr Grimwig, Scrooge, Artful Dodger, Mr M'Choakumchild, Tiny Tim Cratchit. Mervyn Peake, the author of *Gormenghast*, had characters named Titus Groan, Rottcodd, Steerpike and Swelter.

In pairs, ask the students to discuss and write the down the sort of characters that might go with the following names:

Sergei Slimeball	Tina Tippytoes
Whimsy Cottoncloud	Dozy Lie-abed
Grabber Bankroll	Grim Scowler
Mr Jokefest	Tripper Smashemup

Extension

Ask the pairs to have a go at making up names that describe certain characters.

EXPLORING

Abstract art

The students explore the meaning behind abstract works of art.

Groups: 3–4

Time: 10 minutes

Resources: Copies of the abstract artworks on the photocopiable sheet *Abstract art* (p. 139) enlarged to A3 size and pinned up for all the students to see; copies of some of Picasso's abstract paintings, if possible; paper and pencils

What to do

Ask the students to study the pictures and explain to them that each is an abstract representation of something. (If you have some copies of Picasso's work you can show these as examples of this type of art.) They must study the pictures and explore the possible ideas that are being represented. After a set time, call the students together to discuss their interpretations. Ask them what clues they found in the pictures to inform their decisions.

Extension

Ask the students to draw an abstract representation of their classroom with several students included. They should explore how best to represent the various features in the drawing.

EXPLORING

Discover the message

The students explore a series of scraps of paper to work out a message.

Groups: Pairs

Time: 10–15 minutes

Resources: For each pair, a copy of the photocopiable sheet *Discover the message* (p. 143); scissors; paper and pencils

What to do

Give each pair a copy of the message. Explain that it was once a sheet of paper on which a message had been written, but over time it has been damaged and fragmented. They must try and piece the fragments together and work out the original message.

Extension

Ask the pairs to write a message on a piece of paper and then 'distress' it and tear it into eight fragments for another pair to put together and decipher.

EXPLORING

Who saved the day?

The students explore the stories of the potential candidates to decide which is the most convincing.

 Group size: 6

 Time: 20–30 minutes

 Resources: Paper and pencils; whiteboard and pen

What to do

Write the following names and whereabouts on your whiteboard:

- Joe the groom – in the stables.
- Mr Rose the gardener – in the vegetable garden.
- Mrs Moles – a tourist visitor to the house.
- Mrs Maggs the cook – downstairs in the kitchen.
- Mr Evans the estate manager – in his office in the attic.
- Mrs Duster the cleaner – polishing the silver in the dining room on the ground floor.

Explain to the students that a famous painting situated in a private apartment on the first floor was in danger of being damaged by a bird that had fallen down a chimney into the room, but someone had saved it. The students must each take on the role of one of the characters and claim that they saved the painting. Since the apartment was private, they must think of a story that explains what they were doing in that area and how they came to save the painting. Each character can be asked six questions by the other group members to verify their story or explain aspects of it. When all the 'characters' have told their story, the students take a vote to decide which is the most convincing.

Extension

The most convincing story from each group is retold for a class vote.

What a disaster!

The students explore film genres to itemise component parts.

Groups: 4–6

Time: 10–15 minutes

Resources: Paper and pencils

What to do

Explain to the groups that they will have five minutes to think of and write down all the common features of disaster movies, such as a set of different characters, including the more vulnerable young and elderly, and a slow build-up to the disaster with only the film watcher knowing something is going to happen. After five minutes, ask which group has the most features and let them read them out, one at a time. As each feature is read out, the other groups raise their hands if it is included in their lists as well. Each group can then contribute any additional features from their lists.

Extension

Ask the groups to plot the storyline for a new disaster movie, including some of the common features they have explored.

EXPLORING

What happened next?

The students explore possible storylines following on from an introduction.

 Groups: 3–4

 Time: 15 minutes

 Resources: Paper and pencils

What to do

Read the following extract to the students and then ask them to develop the story within their groups. They should talk about what happens next and make notes on the outline of their story.

> The house was larger than I expected and was hidden from view by a dense blanket of undergrowth. I pushed my way through the shrubs and climbed the steps to the front door. I banged the knocker several times, but no one answered. As I stood back and looked up I glimpsed a face at an upstairs window and then it vanished. If there was someone in the house, why weren't they answering the door?

Compare the storylines to see how similar they are and ask the students what initiated their ideas.

Extension

Ask the groups to explore in depth the character of someone from their story, discussing what motivates them and what events in their history have led them to the present situation.

PROJECTS

These projects are designed to be taught over a series of lessons. Students will engage in a variety of different learning skills while completing the projects. They are able to take note of how mastering one learning skill will allow progression to the next, and also how these skills interlink and are needed for all aspects of curriculum engagement.

PROJECTS

A suitable timetable

The students use the skills that they have gained to create a timetable of lessons that will best equip them for working life in the outside world.

Group size: 6

Time: 2 hours

Resources: For each group, the template of a timetable from the photocopiable sheet *A suitable timetable* (p. 144); paper and pencils

What to do

Explain to the students that they are going to devise a timetable of lessons that is designed to teach them the skills they think they will need after school. The timetable will consist of five lessons per day and each subject must have a minimum of two lessons per week. The work involved in this task will utilise the following skills:

Understand: Students must understand the task they have been set and what is required of them to complete it successfully.

Identify: In pairs within their groups, the students discuss the ten most important skills for life after school and note them down.

Describe: Each pair, in turn, describes the skills they have chosen to other members of the group.

Analyse and evaluate: The students discuss the skills suggested and evaluate their importance. They can take a vote on any disagreements or consider ways of amalgamating skills.

Refine: The students refine the list of skills into suitable lessons.

Collate: In their groups, the students collate the lessons and draw up a suitable timetable.

Explore: The groups examine each other's timetables and discuss their values. Ask the students if they would change any of their lessons in light of reading a different timetable.

Creating a children's TV programme

The students create a half-hour television programme for children aged five to eight years. The programme must be character-led and incorporate the same format each time.

Group size: 3–4

Time: 1–2 hours

Resources: Paper and pencils

What to do

Explain to the students that they are going to devise a half-hour TV programme to appeal to children aged five to eight years. The programme must have a main character, which can be an actual person or a cartoon. The same format should be repeated each week, although there can be variations on a theme. The task will involve the following skills:

Understand: The students must understand the task and what is required of them to complete it successfully.

Describe: Each student, in turn, describes their favourite programme when they were the same age as the target group.

Analyse: The students explain what made their favourite programmes so appealing to them.

Identify: The groups discuss and identify the key features of a successful show and write down as many points as possible.

Collate: Each group considers the key features and collates them in order of importance.

Refine: The groups refine their lists into five key points.

Explore: The students explore possible programmes and characters, before making their choice.

Evaluate: Each group, in turn, describes their programme, giving reasons for their choice. Then a whole-class discussion evaluates their potential and, if possible, the students devise a new programme that incorporates the best features of the group programmes.

PROJECTS

A summer event

The students devise a summer event. This could take the form of a music festival, a fete, a sporting event or a grand outdoor party.

Group size: 5–6

Time: 1–2 hours

Resources: Paper and pencils; the internet (if possible)

What to do

Explain that the students are going to plan a summer event within their groups. The task will involve the following skills:

Understand: The students must understand the task and what is required of them to complete it successfully.

Describe: Each group identifies and describes the key features that will make their event successful.

Investigate: If the students have access to a computer, they can investigate features of their chosen event. For example, if they are planning a music festival, they can investigate the bands that are currently popular and what else makes a festival popular, such as food and drink stalls and other acts. If they are planning a sports event, they can investigate what sports are involved and the order in which they take place, along with other sideshows.

Identify: Each group notes down as many features as possible for their chosen event.

Collate: Each group collates their list in order of most important to least important features.

Refine: The groups then refine their lists, choosing ten items to incorporate into their event.

Evaluate: Each group, in turn, describes their event, and the class votes by a show of hands for the event that they think has the most potential to succeed.

The town council project

The students consider the pros and cons of opening a nightclub in a residential area from the viewpoint of different members of the public.

Group size: Pairs

Time: 1+ hour

Resources: Paper and pencils

What to do

Explain to the students that they are to imagine that an entrepreneur wishes to open a nightclub in a residential area. Each pair will be given a different character and they must decide if that character would be for or against the idea. They write down their reasons to take to a town council meeting. Each pair speaks out in character and the class then takes a vote on whether or not to allow the nightclub to be opened. Characters could include: a doctor in A&E, the owner of a brewery, an elderly couple who live close to the site, a drug and alcohol councillor, a fast-food shop owner, a local 20-year-old, a mother of two young children, a refuse collector, the entrepreneur proposing the nightclub, a dancer, the parents of a teenager. The task will involve the following skills:

Understand: The students must understand the task and what is required of them to complete it successfully.

Identify: The students identify the reasons for their character's viewpoint.

Collate and refine: The students collate their reasons and refine them into an argument.

Analyse and explore: The students analyse the various reasons given to explore how valid they consider them.

Evaluate: The students evaluate the arguments to decide whether or not the nightclub should open.

PROJECTS

Designer drink

The students consider and produce strategies to promote a new drink.

 Group size: 4–6

 Time: 1–2 hours

 Resources: The internet; magazines; paper and pencils

What to do

Explain to the students that they must think up a marketing strategy that involves a promotional slogan for a new lime-flavoured, sugar-free fizzy drink. This could be a diet drink, a child's drink or a sports drink. The task will involve the following skills:

Understand: The students must understand the task and what is required of them to complete it successfully.

Identify: The students identify the target audience for the drink.

Describe: They describe what is special and/or appealing about their drink.

Investigate: Each group investigates the marketing strategies of similar drinks online and in magazines.

Analyse and evaluate: Each group analyses the strategies to promote other drinks and evaluates them to decide which they consider would be effective.

Collate and refine: In their groups, students collate all the information about their drink and refine it to produce a suitable marketing slogan.

PHOTOCOPIABLE RESOURCES

Describe and draw

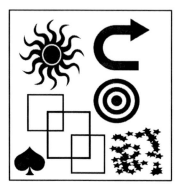

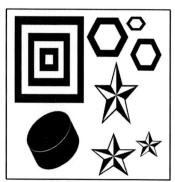

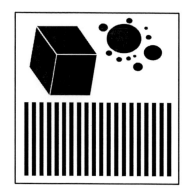

Through asking

Who:

- Has at least one brother?

- Has at least one sister?

- Owns a dog?

- Owns a cat?

- Eats cereal for breakfast?

- Supports a football team?

- Likes tea?

- Likes to play computer games?

- Knows their six times table?

- Can roll their tongue?

- Can tie a tie?

- Knows the capital city of Australia?

- Likes chocolate?

- Has a television in their bedroom?

- Wears a watch?

Making sense

'I prefer The Lemon Tree as I like the cakes there.'

'Where did you go?'

'Just as well, otherwise you might have got very hungry.'

'Yes, especially the brightly coloured spices. Did you find the food too spicy?'

'Good idea. Where shall we go?'

'Hello, you're back from your holiday then?'

'Yes, there are many beautiful temples and everything is very colourful.'

'Okay, that's where we'll go.'

'All that talk of being hungry has made me feel hungry! Do you want to go and have some lunch?'

'Oh hi. Yes, we got home yesterday.'

'We went to India.'

'Nico's does really tasty baguettes.'

'Oh no, I love hot curries.'

'You must have seen some fabulous sights there.'

Check the context

1. I'll have sausage, egg and bucket, please.
2. Someone broke the window throwing a sponge.
3. They make apple juice and dogs from the fruit.
4. That jumper goes very well with those bananas.
5. The birds live in cracks in the rocks and make their nests out of dumplings.
6. We were out in a boat and caught a cow.
7. Close the monkey when you go out.
8. This potato is too complicated to read.
9. The car only had three rivers.
10. I bought this planet in a sale.
11. The grass is looking very greasy.
12. My horse loves eating chicken.
13. The film was very exciting, all about spies and mermaids.
14. I saw trapeze artists and a really funny flower at the circus.
15. The artist painted a landscape of trees and sugar.
16. For this recipe you will need: chicken, onions, carrots and pencils.
17. He galloped the horse up to the sun.
18. She climbed into bed and hid under the flannels.
19. I like cream with beef burgers.
20. The cat curled up in the lettuce.

What's in a dream?

I was walking through a field of wild flowers and a large bird was circling above my head. The sky was blue and the sun was shining brightly. Ahead of me was a steep hill that I had to climb. It was very hard work and I was puffing and panting and feeling tired. As I reached the top of the hill I saw a lake in the distance. The water shimmered in the sunlight. I ran down the hill and dived into the lake and floated on the surface. I continued on my way and came to the entrance of a cave. It was dark inside, pitch black, and I could see nothing. I felt my way along the wall of the cave. My feet felt as though I was walking in treacle. I turned round and left the cave. As I walked along I heard a bird singing and a black cat ran across my path. I came to a house and wanted to go in, but I could not find a door. I walked round the house several times looking for one. Then I saw a huge, wooden door, but it had no handle to open it. I left the house and carried on walking. I could smell something delicious and wanted to eat. I saw plates of mouth-watering food but they vanished every time I got near to them. Suddenly a fog came down. It was thick and clammy and I couldn't see the path. A giant fly buzzed past me, then I saw a giant spider and it chased me. I ran into a giant marshmallow and it began to smother me. I woke up.

Interpret the sign

Story sequence

What can you deduce?

It was windy and cold. It was only two weeks until the Christmas holidays, and Toni was also glad that today was the last day of the school week and she had two days of the weekend to look forward to. She had attended drama club today after school, and now it was dark. She wrapped her coat tighter around her as she walked away from the bus stop and down the country lane to her house. She heard neighing from Mrs Walker's stables and began to run as a slight drizzle started to fall. Finally, she reached her house and walked up the garden path, glad to be home.

Toni fished the key from her bag but, as she tried to put it into the lock, she dropped it on the ground. Oh no! There was no light outside the house. She banged on the door and heard Billy begin to bark, but no one came to let her in. Her two younger brothers would be in the back room on the computer and would not be able to hear the door, but where was her dad? He was usually home by now. She banged even harder, and Billy's barking became much louder but still no one came. She knew her mobile battery was flat too, so she could not even call her dad inside. What a pain!

After five minutes of banging, Toni heard the garden gate open. She turned to see her Uncle Tom and his daughter Nikki coming down the path. They seemed surprised to see her shivering outside the door, but after she explained the situation, Nikki called the family phone with her mobile. A few seconds later Toni's father opened the door, holding some gold tinsel in one hand and a string of coloured lights in the other. He apologised for not hearing Toni's knocking, and ushered them in to the warm, dry house.

Questions

1. Which month does this story occur in?
2. What day does this happen on?
3. What method of transport did Toni use to get back to her village from school?
4. What animals does Mrs Walker own?
5. What animal is Billy?
6. Is Toni the oldest or the youngest child in the family?
7. Is there a telephone in the house?
8. How are Toni and Nikki related?
9. What had Toni's dad been doing in the house?

© Activities to Develop Learning Skills at KS3 LDA

What's happened?

Study the picture

Study the picture – questions

1. What is trying to steal a bread roll?
2. How many ducklings are on the pond?
3. What has the girl on the swing lost?
4. How many dogs are there all together?
5. What is the logo on the park-keeper's sweatshirt?
6. What's happened to the boy in the striped bobble hat?
7. Who is going down the slide?
8. What shouldn't be in the pond?
9. What has the lady in the spotty dress bought?
10. What are the man and boy in matching jumpers doing?
11. What is the old lady on the bench feeding?
12. How many wheels are there all together in the park?
13. What is upsetting the football game?
14. What is the man in the flat cap pushing?
15. What is the girl with the plaits sitting on?
16. What is a lady pointing at?
17. What must you not do?
18. How many birds are there all together?
19. Who's in a hurry?
20. What is directly above the clubhouse?

Who likes what?

Name	Chips	Burger	Chicken	Fish	Coleslaw	Beans	Salad	Cola	Juice	Smoothie	Milkshake
Ahmed	✓	✓	✓	✗	✓	✓	✗	✗	✗	✗	✓
Ben	✗	✓	✗	✓	✓	✗	✓	✓	✓	✓	✗
Chloe	✗	✗	✓	✗	✗	✓	✗	✓	✓	✓	✓
Danny	✓	✗	✓	✓	✓	✓	✗	✗	✓	✓	✗
Enrique	✓	✓	✓	✗	✗	✓	✗	✓	✗	✓	✗
Frazer	✓	✗	✓	✗	✗	✓	✓	✗	✗	✓	✓
Georgia	✗	✓	✓	✗	✓	✓	✗	✓	✗	✗	✓
Harry	✗	✗	✓	✗	✓	✗	✓	✓	✓	✓	✗
Iqbal	✓	✓	✗	✗	✗	✓	✗	✗	✓	✗	✓
Johnny	✓	✗	✓	✓	✗	✗	✓	✗	✓	✗	✓
Kelisha	✓	✓	✗	✓	✓	✓	✗	✓	✗	✗	✗
Le'bron	✓	✓	✓	✗	✓	✗	✗	✗	✓	✓	✗
Maya	✗	✓	✗	✗	✗	✓	✗	✓	✓	✗	✓
Nishan	✗	✗	✓	✗	✗	✓	✓	✓	✗	✗	✗
Oscar	✗	✗	✗	✓	✗	✓	✓	✓	✗	✓	✗

Sort them out

An eye of newt and two snail shells.
Four ounces of sugar – caster is best.
Do not clamp the frame during transportation.
Buses will leave for the town every half hour.
These parrots are wild and may bite.

The same amount of butter softened at room temperature.
Make sure that your helmet meets required safety standards.
Three fingers from an old and wizened elf.
Keep this side of the barrier at all times.
The pool is open from 9am until 9pm.

Look out for cars, pedestrians and other obstacles.
An adder's tongue and the wart of a toad.
Two eggs, organic are best if you can get them.
This is a restricted area for keepers only.
Lunch and dinner are served in the Sunshine Hall.

Don't feed sweets or any food to the monkeys.
Ten giant's toenails, hard and yellow.
Check the handlebar and stem, wheels and brakes.
When you arrive, check in at reception.
A large tablespoonful of currants or raisins.

There is a disco and dance competition on Saturday night.
A dozen moth wings, brown and mottled.
Changes to your bicycle can make it unsafe.
Don't bang on the glass as it frightens the animals.
Four ounces of flour, sieved.

Abstract art

Spot the difference

Spot the difference

I would rather

I would rather have an ice cream than an ice lolly.

I would rather go skiing than sunbathe.

I would rather meet a crocodile than a tiger.

I would rather eat cabbage than a Brussels sprout.

I would rather fly in an aeroplane than sail in a ship.

I would rather eat a cake than chips.

I would rather find a spider than a mouse in my bed.

I would rather have purple hair than green hair.

I would rather parachute jump than bungee jump.

I would rather dance than sing.

I would rather have a spot on my nose than a corn on my toe.

I would rather be invisible than be able to fly.

I would rather explore space than the bottom of the sea.

I would rather look after dolphins than orangutans.

I would rather watch a clown than an acrobat.

I would rather bathe in custard than baked beans.

Discover the message

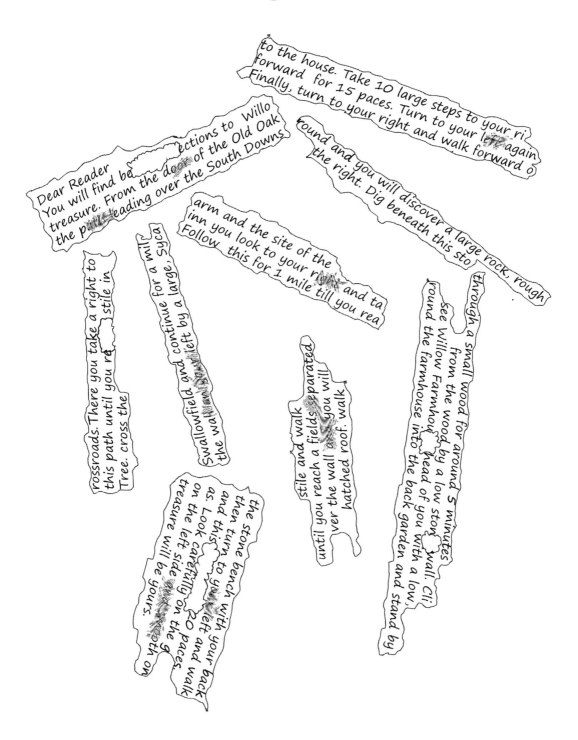

A suitable timetable

Monday				
Tuesday				
Wednesday				
Thursday				
Friday				